T0370517

A Look at
Grief

Donna Spicer Roberts

AuthorHouse™
1663 Liberty Drive
Bloomington, IN 47403
www.authorhouse.com
Phone: 1 (800) 839-8640

Published by AuthorHouse 11/08/2018

ISBN: 978-1-5462-6349-4 (sc)
ISBN: 978-1-5462-6348-7 (e)

Library of Congress Control Number: 2018911933

Print information available on the last page.

authorHOUSE®

A LOOK AT

GRIEF

So, we fix our eyes not on what is seen, but on what is unseen, for what is seen is temporary, but what is unseen is eternal.

—2 Corinthians 4:18

"Brothers" Acrylic

This painting of my twin grandsons, Austin and Clayton, was inspired by a photo their mother had taken of them while they were vacationing in Florida. At fifteen, they were regular kids and full of energy. The quiet moment between them touched my heart. I knew I wanted to recreate through paint on canvas, that slice of time: to look at, touch, and relive. *"In quietness and trust is your strength."* **Isaiah 30:15**

It was Easter Sunday, March 27, 2016. The boys had spent spring break at home as they had just gotten their driver's licenses and first jobs. They were a few weeks away from their seventeenth birthday. Life was good and going rather smoothly. Everyone in the family was busy with other things, so we skipped our usual Easter get together.

I went to bed around ten p.m. and had fallen asleep while watching tv. I awakened later and vaguely noticed the time was after midnight. I was about to doze off, when my phone rang. My heart responded immediately to the intrusive sound. Late night calls alarm me; usually for good reason. The incoming call was from Clayton. When I answered, the response was screaming, muffled shouting, and louder screams. A tiny speck of sanity allowed me to ask, "What's wrong?" He was breathless and hysterical but eventually told me, "Austin's not breathing!"

The hours that followed are somewhat of a blur to me now. I know that hell exists on earth as I watched and experienced the surreal time unfold at the hospital. There are no words to describe this horrific night.

"We couldn't save him," someone said. Or, words to that effect. I quit listening and breathing. Time seemed to stop. Reality changed. My surroundings appeared warped. Everything was moving in slow motion, but my mind could still not keep up. Our new world was being created; a hideous thing that grabbed me and pulled me downward. Oh God, please let me wake up from this nightmare!

This written and visual look at my grief evolved from the suggestion of my grief counselor. During my numerous visits, she encouraged me to write and paint what I was feeling.

I balked at the idea of writing. It was difficult to organize my thoughts and seemed pointless to write about how miserable I felt. Painting required too much effort those sickening months following his death. My desire to be creative was gone. Life had been reduced to the basics. Getting out of bed was an accomplishment. This is where I set my bar. Anything beyond that could be viewed as productive. To say I was grieving is an understatement. I was grief. It's a wonder I survived the first six months after Austin's death, as I am getting on in years. I was lucky to have support from family and friends and continue to benefit from those relationships.

As I look back now, I know it was our loving God through Christ who picked me up from the hospital floor that horrible night, and carried me until I was strong enough to walk on my own. During the last two years, a spiritual quest and awakening grew from this overwhelming loss that is beyond description. There was a spark within that kept me going. A voice that said, "Yes, you can move; you can face another day."

April 27, 2016

My immediate goal is just to get through the day. The loss of our sweet boy, Austin, is unbearable. It has been almost a month since he lost his life to a senseless accident. My heart breaks every day. I feel like the very part of me that makes me a whole person is gone. I no longer feel like I'll ever live with any joy. Nothing interests me. I try to lean on God, but my cluttered mind has trouble holding on to abstract thoughts. I want very much to feel peace; to know without a doubt that I'll see Austin again. I will read and meditate on God. I concentrate on feeling

His presence around me. I know that I must practice this every day, but days like yesterday were spent immersed in every negative thought I could find in my mind. It wasn't hard to see all the failures I've had in my life. All the bad decisions, disappointments, and heart wrenching losses.

April 29, 2016

Life Sucks!!!! Life stinks. I hate my life!!! I can't stand not having Austin here. I miss him so much! Everything hurts. Life is too hard. I can't stand my life without Austin. My boy. Sometimes when I'm sleeping, I awaken because I feel something on the bed; like he was sitting there with me. I miss him so much I can't bear it. Why did this have to happen?!!!

April 30, 2016

The emptiness I feel continues. I hope I don't try to fill it with unhealthy choices. Eating too much. Drinking too much; the extra glass. I don't want to fill it with regret. Regret for everything I perceive Austin will miss; was cheated out of. I don't want to fill the emptiness with disappointment. Every disappointment and all the regrets I've had in my life want to crowd into my grief-filled mind. It's too much!

I pray the hole in my heart, the emptiness, will scab over. That nothing will fill it. It's Austin's place. His spot. Nothing can replace the loss I feel for our boy.

May 1, 2016

Today is the first day of a new month. I will focus on living this day in the present. I am going to live in the moment so I can feel God's presence more clearly. I will not worry about the future or have regrets about the past. This will be hard for me.

Search me, O God, and know my anxious thoughts. **Psalm 139:23**

June 23, 2016

Oh, the optimism of May 1. This pain is crushing me. The realness of Austin being gone from us is overwhelming to look at. I'm angry, sad, depressed, and hopeless. I don't want to be around other people. I'm jealous of what looks like "care free" lives. I would like to punch a hole in my wall, jump into it, and disappear.

November 28, 2016

DITTO! I HATE MY LIFE.

September 12, 2017

I have two hummingbirds that dart and dash around the feeder on my patio. In a way, they remind me of my grandsons, Austin and Clayton. These tiny birds seem to fly in harmony but also compete for space. Today, only one hummingbird has shown up.

The remnants of a hurricane in the gulf arrived this morning. But, the fury has turned gentle as the wind rustles the foliage, and rain falls softly to the ground. My heart aches.

September 13, 2017

This day is cool and gray. The sky's color is poking through more of the trees' greenery. Summer is slowly giving up its steamy, hot grip. I am greeting another day of my new life. Nearly a year and a half of holding on. Some days bearable and productive. Others, paralyzingly painful. A thick fog covers my reality.

O, Lord, take me by the hand and comfort me. Please allow your love to penetrate the fog and lift me up.

September 14, 2017

A sunny morning is presenting itself to me. The world is slowly spinning on its predictable path around the sun. I am following my predictable, morning path.

Routines are comforting as they give me a sense of order. Strong coffee, quiet reflection. Taking in the sounds of a new day. Geese squawking as they fly in instinctive formation across the blue sky.

Only God knows what lies ahead of us. I will give it my best shot. I will try to lift my heart from its predictable, sad place this morning.

September 17, 2017

Summer is making the most of its last days. Heat, humidity, and mosquitoes. The gradual shift from summer to fall can be a melancholy time. The bright colors of summer fade away. Autumn's palette will be more subdued with eventual brilliant accents of orange, red, and gold. Nature seems to be putting on the brakes; slowing down.

Those involved in fall sports are happy to be tailgating and comparing teams. I could care less. I see the beginning of fall rituals and the looming holiday season. Now, I dread the times that brought me pleasure. Will my heart ever become adjusted to the life we have? I doubt it. My heart doesn't want to let go. I want to wake up to my old life every morning, but I am a spectator now. I get to watch as it goes on around me. Doesn't life know it left me behind?

September 18, 2017

My heart doesn't feel as heavy today. Normally on awakening, grayness floods my mind. Gray skies regardless of the weather. As an artist, I see gray as a non-color. An even drabness that changes the mood.

Take advantage of a little time that doesn't feel oppressive and overwhelming. A break from darkness feels somewhat hopeful, even if it only lasts a little while.

September 19, 2017

My hummingbirds have grown over the summer. The tiny bodies of spring have turned into miniature "drones." They know where to find a steady source of nourishment. I will miss them when they fly away for the winter.

Every day I have to face reminders of my former life. Sometimes, I hurt so badly that I almost feel sick. Like my hummingbirds, I am learning how to find nourishment for my mind and heart. I have grown stronger physically and somewhat stronger mentally.

Adjusting to tragedies that blindside us seems impossible. I miss my old life so much, but while I was living it, I saw room for improvement. Now in my new life, I realize how vulnerable we are; that our lives dangle from a very thin thread.

God knows my heart. I am being nourished daily by his love. What more can I do?

*For now, we see through a glass darkly; but then face to face:
now I know in part; but then I shall know even as I am known.*

—1 Corinthians 13:12 (KIV)

"Harmony" Acrylic

September 20, 2017

"Grief wave" is a term used to describe a sudden feeling of loss that hits without warning. A memory may flash before you that has been triggered by one of the senses: a fragrance, a song, a newly discovered picture. There are endless possibilities. A grief wave may be gentle bringing a tear, or a tsunami that knocks you down, and drowns you in sorrow.

God designed the human mind and body to be resilient. My aging mind and body have had numerous setbacks. But I keep going on. To what? I will ponder this today.

Where can I go from your Spirit? Where can I flee from your presence? If I go up to the heavens, you are there; if I make my bed in the depths, you are there. If I rise on the wings of the dawn, if I settle on the far side of the sea, even there your hand will guide me, your right hand will hold me fast.

—Psalm 139:7-10

"At Low Tide" Pastel

September 21, 2017

These last days of September are still warm, but some of my plants look tired as if they have expended all of their energy. The life cycle is brutally consistent. The foliage of the trees will brighten to brilliant colors. The grand finale of the season. I resemble my tired plants; not the beauty of fall. I'm worn out from grief and the unfairness of life.

Am I an annual or a perennial? I'll wait until spring to decide.

September 22, 2017

I have set the Lord always before me. Because he is at my right hand, I will not be shaken. **Psalm 16:18**

"*I will not be shaken.*" I read those words and wish they would penetrate my mind where doubt and fear do constant battle with peace and trust. Some days, I feel like the slightest nudge from an outside source would topple me like a row of carefully placed dominoes. Life feels precarious. Yet, I think I've seen the worst.

How can I not survive anything life drops on me? I pray that I'm not given the chance to test this theory.

September 25, 2017

There are days when I feel like indulging in self-pity and spending an hour crying myself out. My heart aches so much for what has been lost and what could have been. Cruel, cruel life.

Each morning, as I awaken, my mental state is in a dark hole. I either stay there or try to crawl out. This takes enormous effort. Grief has total control of my life now. Is this my new reality?

Humble yourselves, therefore, under God's almighty hand, that he may lift you up in due time. Cast all your anxiety on him because he cares for you. **1 Peter 5:6-7**

September 29, 2017

Every day, I look for ways to lift myself up; to try and not look at or feel the empty part of my heart. I read, pray, and meditate. I've rearranged furniture and painted walls. There isn't a cluttered closet or messy drawer safe from my busy hands.

I'm listening, God, trying to hear you. Please speak louder because my sorrow overpowers your voice.

Deep calls unto deep at the noise of your waterfalls; all your waves and billows have gone over me. **Psalm 41:7**

October 3, 2017

Today was a good day for a walk around our neighborhood lake. I haven't spent much time there since "It" happened. I remember when the boys were little, we would go there often. They enjoyed chasing the somewhat docile geese. Sometimes, a cranky bird would chase after them. We laughed a lot and enjoyed being together.

Now, I have to make myself do things I know will cause my heart to ache. This place, the lake, is full of so many happy memories. I want to be there. I am filled with such longing though, at these times. Longing for the life we had and for the future we lost.

All my longings lie open before you Lord; my sighing is not hidden from you.

—Psalm 38:9

"Yesterday's Reflection" Pastel

October 6, 2017

In Tennessee, October is more summer than autumn. The leaves are falling but perhaps from habit, not cooler temperatures.

We all have habits. Even animals. Now that my daily life has changed dramatically, I have to create new habits. This dull feeling of sadness and loss upon awakening each day is becoming a habit. Praying to God for help and strength follows. Better habit.

Will I know again, feeling pleasant and rested when I open my eyes after a night's sleep? To be content just feeling okay? OK. That is my standard answer when someone asks, "How are you?" But my OK is not okay at all.

October 9, 2017

Yesterday, our little family met for lunch to celebrate a birthday. Now, when our family gets together I feel loss more intensely. I want to be with my family, but it hurts. As I look at those whom I love so dearly, I see Austin there too, but he's NOT there. He is forever NOT there. I look at my son and others and know they are hurting also, but we carry on. Life goes on, as they say. Yeah, right! I'm ruined. Broken. Unfixable. What's left of Donna goes on in robotic fashion. Doing what needs to be done. Now, I must fold laundry.

October 11, 2017

Yesterday was a difficult day. The trickle from the dike walling up my grief became little waves of pain ebbing and flowing throughout the day. On days like this, I must exhibit self-control so I won't appear unhinged. Tears, always so close to the surface.

"Go out and grab what you can from your old life. And live in the present and grab the greatness from it too." Words of encouragement from a friend. Well-intentioned advice, but grief looks different when you're not in it. Grief can feel complicated. It obscures the past and taints the present. The present HURTS. I know tomorrow is going to hurt also.

"Lean on, trust in and be confident in the Lord with all your heart and mind and do not rely on your own understanding." **Psalm 3:5**

October 13, 2017

Ecclesiastes 2:12-17 *"Now I began a study of the comparative studies of wisdom and folly, and anyone else would come to the same conclusion I did—that wisdom is of more value than foolishness, just as light is better than darkness; for the wise man sees, while the fool is blind. And yet I noticed that there was one thing that happened to wise and foolish alike—just as the fool will die, so will I. So what value is all of my wisdom? Then I realized that even wisdom is futile. For the wise and the fool both die, and in the days to come both will be long forgotten. So now I hate life because it is all so irrational; all is foolishness, chasing the wind."*

Being perplexed and disillusioned with life is certainly not a new concept.

October 14, 2017

O, Lord, lift me up from my "sad place." My reality. Take me by the hand and show me your love. Help me see the beauty around me. Lift the gray fog that shrouds my world now. Please help me remember you are always with me. Forgive me when I say I hate my life. Please quell my need to know "why." Why Austin?

Why? Lord, it's hard to accept this new life. It doesn't feel like life at all. Life means hope, renewal, energy. I'm a body and mind going through the motions of life. I know you don't want this for me. Please help me learn to surrender my hopelessness to you and meet you in the present where you wait for me.

October 15, 2017

"And surely I am with you always, to the very end of the age." **Matthew 28:20**

Grief is a lonely place. I live there; for it does seem to have a life of its own. No matter where I am or what I am doing, it follows me. Relentlessly. My constant companion, grief, in one way or another will be with me for a very long time. Grief feels lonely because it is totally yours. No one can fathom its depth but Christ.

Recently, while talking about my loss, someone said, "Life goes on." Really? Of course, it does for you. You can't see into my broken world. No, "life" doesn't go on for some of us who have lost so much. Yes, I'm still here. I am alive and physically well, but I feel that I'm more of an observer rather than a participant in life.

October 17, 2017

My busy life did not allow time to write yesterday. Busy life. Busy trying to hide from my present life. No matter what I do to stay active, from being productive to spending time with family or friends, I feel like half of me is involved. I'm functioning in life with half of who I was. It's like trying to ride a bike with one leg. My balance is way off. The slightest push or nudge, and I fall over. There is no zest for living. The world or life I spent all these years building is no longer here. When I look at it now, I just think, "What the hell is this?" It isn't hell—it's just my "sad place." Now, I must get "busy."

"Observant" Pastel

October 18, 2017

"Fear not for I am with you; be not dismayed for I am your God. I will strengthen you...." **Isaiah 41**

Lord, I thought my life would smooth out in the later years; that life's roller coaster would have less breathless plunges that leave you gasping and holding on to the ride. Do I have to wait until my life is over for peace? I know you offer your peace to me moment by moment. However, the noise of grief drowns out your voice. Lord, help me hear you more clearly. Please wrap your everlasting love around me and reassure me.

I know you are on the ride with me, Lord. Please hold on to me.

October 19, 2017

God is the creator of life, but with life there is also death. Everything that lives, eventually dies. I want to blame God for Austin's death, but where does that actually take me? Then, do I blame God for everything that doesn't go my way? Where does this stop?

Every time we love, we open up like a flower. Beautiful, but vulnerable. A leap of faith that comes so naturally. We do not choose whom to love. Our hearts dictate that. We know in our minds there is a beginning and an ending. Our hearts will not listen to practicality. Our hearts prefer, "forever."

October 20, 2017

"Lord, why are you standing aloof and far away? Why do you hide when I need you the most?.....Why do you ignore my cries for help?" **Psalm 10 and 22**

How many times have I said to myself, "I don't understand." "Why?" Why now? Why our boy with his whole life to live? Why do you allow us to endure unimaginable loss?

I can't feel your presence because my pain over-shadows you. My faith wavers during a daily battle with grief. I can go on fighting with my grief, trying to gain ground. To topple it; to push it away. Or, I can give up trying to make sense of any of this madness.

October 21, 2017

A crisp, fall morning. A day to be thankful for God's gift of another day. A tenuous gift. A gift that can quickly turn into a never-ending nightmare. I yearn for those days when I could look out my window and see life. My old life. The view from my window is still the same, but the viewer has different eyes. How can my world be in disarray, but nothing I see is changed?

Just as I feel a tiny adjustment to the new life, it passes. Then, I am right back in the heaviness of loss. The reality of the "changed life" sinks in deeper saying to me, "Yes, Donna, this really happened." I can't hide from it. I know it follows me wherever I go......even into my dreams.

The Lord has said, "My Presence will go with you, and I will give you rest." I will take a large dose of that today, God. Thank you.

October 22, 2017

To this end I labor, struggling with all his energy, which so powerfully works in me. **Colossians 1:29**

Every day, I struggle with this grief. My grief. I look to God to infuse me with strength. God's energy is powerful, but each day I awaken with the same weakness of spirit. When I open my eyes, the gray fog is there, waiting for me. Oh, yes, this is my life now. A hideous mutation of what once seemed a normal life. I've seen many ups and downs during my time here on earth. I've wanted to believe that I've become stronger from my experiences. Nothing can prepare you for this kind of loss.

October 23, 2017

I have felt so irritable today. Feeling like crap is a way of life now. Some days it affects me physically. I just want our boy back! I want to see him standing in front of my fridge threatening to drink milk from the carton. Then, laughing at my horrified face. His laugh. His smile and voice. The uniqueness of him. His bear hugs.

Well-meaning people say, "He is in a better place." I cringe at these words. The well-wishers would want their dearly loved child safe at home with them. That sounds way better than in the obscure afterworld. Yes, I do believe the eternity God has planned for us is real. That knowledge is built into my faith. I know my spirit will be with my loved ones after I die, but it's now that concerns me. I want our boy here with us now! We were cheated out of our earthly life with him. There are no words or platitudes that can make this hideous reality easier to accept.

How can I stand this? This life without our boy.

October 25, 2017

But as for me, I watch in hope for the Lord, I wait for God, my savior; my God will hear me. **Micah 7:7**

You are getting an earful today, Lord. I'm pissed! This life is too hard! I've had more than my share of loss. I find it most difficult to slip into divine thinking when I am suffering. "Learn to live above your circumstances." Really? I have trouble wrapping my mind around this concept. I want to lift myself up, but how is this possible when I've lost so much?

"I pour out my complaints before him and tell him my troubles. For I am overwhelmed. **Psalm 142:2-3a (NLT)**

October 28, 2017

The sun is shining brightly today, and all seem well. There are moments or small passages of time where my mind is away from its "sad place." A feeling of normalcy flashes before me. Then, my mind says, "No, this is not your world. Your world has totally changed." I don't want to feel normal without Austin. It's like letting go of him. I can't. It's as if holding on to him will keep us in the past, and this horrible thing will not be real. These are very unsettling feelings.

October 29, 2017

A new day. An opportunity for growth. Or, a day to be pissed about my new life. I must find a different word to describe my life. New, has a connotation of freshness, hopefulness. I feel neither of these. Crappy life, comes to mind, but that puts me in a very negative place with no hope. I really don't expect to outlive my sadness. it's always there reminding me of my loss. My family's loss.

Our twins lit up the room when we were together. They were life! A magnet. A force that you could feel. The boys. The fellas.

Oh God, how cruel to lose our boy.

October 30, 2017

…..When I was in great need he saved me. **Psalm 116:6**

I fully believe these words. I know had I not reached out to God for help daily, I would be in a vastly different spot, mentally. This pain is too much to bear on my own. I do feel stronger today. The sadness persists, though it doesn't overwhelm me as it has previously. Could I have a setback? Perhaps. I am resolved to staying busy. Being productive.

November 3, 2017

A light rain is falling. At this moment, I feel bland. The holidays are looming closer, and as I'm out and about, the stores are announcing the forced gaiety of the season. Some of us don't feel the urgency to be happy and shop, shop, shop. I would like to skip the entire ordeal. The last Christmas for me was 2015. A memorable time with my entire family. Seeing our family without Austin, leaves me feeling empty and very sad. But, I put on my "happy face," and soldier my way through. Onward Christian soldier. Stay in step. Do what you always do.

November 8, 2017

A gray day and a gray mood. It is so difficult to lift myself up most days. Projects, tasks, and socializing help, but the grayness lingers. This is my life now.

I will try harder not to feel hopeless as I pray for strength. What lies ahead? Do not think about the future. Today is where your thoughts belong. When they go to the past, I am overwhelmed with sorrow and loss. Its grip is strong and enduring. The future is just the calendar; endless days, each with its own mystery.

Humans are so obsessed with the future. "One more day, please," we say, hopefully.

November 9, 2017

Well, the sun is out today. That helps. I have been keeping very busy with projects around the house. Something to take my mind off of my Loss. To help me cope. What does it mean, "to cope?" Is it accepting one's difficulty and moving forward with it in tow? Keeping it at bay? Does it include really looking at it?

When we cope, are we shutting down the emotional turmoil inside of us? Are we putting off feeling devastation? Who wants to feel that? No wonder we "cope."

Is coping God's way of preventing us from "losing it?" Turning the corner, flipping out. Going crazy. I have felt all of these things to some degree.

I'm not coping well. But no one has to know that.

November 11, 2017

"I believed so I said, I am completely ruined!" **Psalm 116:10 (NCV)**

I say to myself that I am ruined; that life is tainted. Future experiences will have to filter through this stain. What a depressing thought. How much control does my mind have over my broken heart? Can my mind say, "Enough! Snap out of it!" Feeling blessed and having joy; out of reach for me. This bleak outlook of my life could become a self-fulfilling prophecy.

Will the heaviness of my grief lessen with time? My past experiences with grief tell me, yes. For this to happen, though, I must completely acknowledge my loss. By acknowledging, then it confirms what I still do not want to believe. He is gone.

November 13, 2017

"Where then is my hope---who can see any hope for me?" **Job 17:15**

Hope is something that slips away in grief. What is there to hope for? My loved one is gone. I hope I see him again. I hope for heaven or whatever wonders that lie ahead.

I must open up my heart to hope. I have overwhelming feelings of hopelessness. What's the use? My life sucks now. This doesn't help me. I am here. I must have hope somewhere in my heart.

"Hope deferred makes the heart sick, but a longing fulfilled is the tree of life."

—Proverbs 13:12

"Prairie's Repose" Acrylic

November 14, 2017

Every time I wake up from a night's sleep my first thought is: Oh, yes, this is my life now. Then, a dreary feeling washes over me. A moment or two passes as I reconcile myself to this life I am in now. It apparently hasn't woven itself into my being as this has been a daily occurrence for one year and eight months.

I regret that I didn't fully appreciate my old life while I was in it. It's so easy to be lulled into a false sense of security. I had it all but couldn't consistently appreciate it. Why do we strive for more? Unable to feel completely contented. Oh, what I would give to have just one day of that imperfect life back.

November 15, 2017

Today is overcast and rainy. My thoughts are as gloomy as the sky. It feels as though a lifetime of grief has pilled on top of me. There are some respites, but the heaviness is always there. I catch myself wondering, "What if this is a bad dream, and I'll wake up to my old life?" I think about what I've lost, then I think about what Austin lost. Why did God put humans in a world to just die?

The more I try to make sense of things, the more convinced I become of no answers. Period. There is no escaping the pain of loss. Another day to carry the load. Maybe one day it will feel lighter.

"......*Now I know in part; then I shall know fully even as I am fully known.* **1 Corinthians 13:12**

November 16, 2017

My grief. It seems to have taken up permanent residence in my head. I am allowing grief to devour me. Grief stretches out in front of me. This is a lonely and depressing path.

Why do I bother to get out of bed in the morning? I am going through the motions of life, but I am not living. Yes, I am breathing and able to do my tasks each day, but I am not participating in life. I am unable to let God through Christ guide me in the present. I am overwhelmed with what was and what will never be. I cannot change this. No matter how much I cry and how much I drag myself around.

"*My comfort in my suffering is this: Your promise preserves my life.*" **Psalm 119:30**

November 18, 2017

This morning the sky is solid gray. Not dark and stormy, but an even gray with no rays of sun poking through. The wind is whipping the leaves and pine needles into a frenzy as they swirl and fly in every direction. The usual, peaceful sound of my wind chimes has turned frantic, as they struggle to remain vertical.

There is something about the wind. I am mesmerized by its effect on what it touches. Maybe I'm hoping it is God's way of blowing away my fears and cares. *"The wind blows wherever it pleases. You hear its sound, but you cannot tell where it comes from or where it is going. So, it is of everyone born of the spirit."* **John 3:8.**

The wind wants to rearrange things. If it could only reach my mind and rearrange my thoughts. They have been relentlessly consistent.

November 20, 2017

The lead ball and chain of grief that I have been dragging around for one year and eight months feels somewhat lighter. Regardless of whether the weight of it is shifting, or, its grip is loosening, I'll take it. Maybe I'm just worn out.

The holidays. Here they come with their promise of good cheer. Right. What an awkward and difficult time for those of us who is missing a dearly loved one. One less plate to set out. Five grandchildren seen at the table instead of six.

Oh, my heart! How can you stand this?

November 22, 2017

Grief has found a way to bring me back to the basics. With this realization, I have begun thinking more about my relationship with God. Before Austin passed from this life, my faith was motivated by fear. I would pray when I was afraid or fearful of some imagined or real problem. It was totally about me. I never once took into consideration God's expectation of me. My desperation has motivated me to get real with God. To look deeper. Serious life events can draw us closer to God. This horrible tragedy has forced me to realize that I need God in my life daily. Moment by moment.

November 24, 2017

Yesterday, our family gathered at my home for Thanksgiving. I did think about being thankful. Not an easy task when one so loved is not sitting at our table anymore. Austin and Clayton, always filling the room with laughter, pranks, and silliness. Their shared presence was almost palpable. We all fed off of their combined energy.

What is left now? How do we go on? Acting as though nothing has happened? We go on. We just do. What else is there? Even though our hearts are broken, they still keep beating. Our lives go on.

Grief, loss......still with me, shadowing my every move.

November 28, 2017

Well, I feel like crap today. When I begin to gain ground, it turns into quicksand, and I feel myself being pulled downward. This a hell of a way to live. I feel like throwing in the towel and giving up. Why am I trying to feel better? Things I have been doing to help myself such as: reading, studying, praying, meditating, working out, time with friends and family. What's the use? I am ruined. Why not just face it? Accept it. Surrender to it. Perhaps, I will always feel this way.

This is my life now. At least I'm old. I have more days behind me than in front of me. When I was young, I used to wonder how it would feel to know your life was approaching its winter. Well, as it turns out, I don't really give a damn.

Why you don't even know what will happen tomorrow. What is your life? You are a mist that appears for a little while then vanishes. **James:4-14**

December 13, 2017

A few weeks have passed since I have written in this journal of my grieving process. Process: a series of steps or actions taken in order to achieve a particular end. Well, since grieving never really ends for one we love so dearly, it can't be called a process.

I am changed. The former "me" will not return, ever. I must realize this at some point and let go of her. She is gone. A part of me died with Austin.

Dear God, it is hard to let go. Little by little. My mind knows this, but my heart is stubborn. My heart longs for our old life. LIFE! Not good-bye.

December 14, 2017

Yay, I woke up alive again today. Whoopy Doo! Another day to fill with meaningless tasks. I must find some meaning or importance in life again. It has felt hopelessly empty for all of these days since our boy left.

I sound as though I have no one left to love. Take one of our children away, and I'm ready to give up on life. What about those who are still here? I love all of my grandchildren and sons equally. I feel as though I am cheating my grandchildren, as I try to hide my withdrawal from life. I worry they will see through the façade. That they will think I must have loved Austin more than I love them. Hopefully, they are so busy with their lives they don't even notice. I'm the one who thinks too much.

Christmas is around the corner. That I do not want to think about.

December 15, 2017

Eventually, we all have to accept something we cannot change. Acceptance is the hardest part of grief. I am beginning this very difficult process. It can't be forced but must evolve naturally. I consider acceptance a process since a result is hopefully achieved. I have denied acceptance entry into my mind and heart because there's no going back from it. I haven't fully moved out of my home in denial. I still have trouble saying Austin is dead. Just writing the words is difficult. A tiny speck in my mind still wants to believe this can't possibly be true.

The practical part of my mind knows that it's time to deal with this reality. Like a child learning to walk, I take baby steps forward, but eventually fall back into the past. I'm getting up more often than before and taking more little steps. I do not have the resilience and energy of a child learning to walk. My stamina is low.

These days since Austin died have been the hardest, saddest, and loneliest days of my life. God didn't promise us lives of rainbows and unicorns. Problems and pain are part of life.

"Our Father refreshes us on the journey with some pleasant inns, but will not encourage us to mistake them for home." **C. S. Lewis**

December 16, 2017

I call them emotional land mines. They are planted everywhere. You never know when you will trip the wire. It does feel like a battle within myself. As I've been told, "It serves no purpose to give in to painful memories." What about other memories or reminders? Ones that grab ahold of your heart and squeeze until it breaks again.

If I live long enough, I will be able to look at my former life with Austin and smile without sadness. Not today.

"And the day came when the risk to remain tight in the bud was more painful than the risk it took to blossom." —**Anais Nin**

December 17, 2017

My constant companion, grief, follows me through the day and into the night. Nights can become something to fear. When I turn off the light and darkness envelopes me, I have to will myself not to think. There is moderate success, but last night, not so much.

While waiting to fall asleep, a vivid memory appeared. It was Austin's father as a six-year old, wearing a superman costume I had made for him. He loved running, cape flying, pretending to be a super hero. Fast forward to the grieving father, helpless to save his son. The carefree child's face is now one that belies unimaginable pain.

As a parent of older sons, I still want to protect them. To take away heartache; to fix the unfixable. To be a super hero.

December 18, 2017

One week from today is Christmas. Our second Christmas without Austin. Last year I went through December on auto pilot, doing most of the things I normally do…. I think. I've tried to recall some of it, but it's mostly a blur as now one day just dissolves into another.

"Merry Christmas!" I hear from all directions. This cheerful greeting falls flat on me. I know people mean well, but I haven't felt "merry" for over a year and a half.

This week I will stay out of the merriment as much as I can. I'm avoiding people. Self-pity? So what! Grief doesn't go on break over the holidays. On the contrary. Holiday grief can feel overwhelming. Every ornament, Christmas song, movie, or decoration have memories attached. Memories are everywhere I look. No wonder I want to hide.

When I do mange some pleasant times, there is that tap on my shoulder. "Remember me? I own you now," says grief, my constant companion.

December 19, 2017

"Time heals all wounds." How often have I heard that worn out phrase? Yes, it does heal most wounds. However, when you're the one needing your wound healed, time seems to be traveling in slow motion. The days are passing quickly, but time's magical healing power is moving very slowly for me.

I know it's not easy for friends or acquaintances to relate to one who is grieving. Fear of saying the wrong thing can make some conversations awkward. We may be avoided as we, perhaps, make others uncomfortable. And there is this: We are a reminder that shit happens. And it could happen to them also. An unsettling thought, no doubt.

December 20, 2017

This week is dragging by. As people are rushing here and there shopping, partying, baking goodies, and all that comes the week before Christmas, I withdraw. As if that helps. I know that not everyone is relishing this week of December. There are many who feel left out, unable to join the celebration; estrangement, illness, financial woes. And on and on.

I really hate it when I immerse myself in this grief. Wading through the thickness of it. Letting it decide the direction of my day.

"………But the mind controlled by the Spirit is life and peace…" **Romans 8:6**

December 21, 2017

The sun is deliberately hiding for the third day in a row. When the weather reflects the tone of my mind and heart, I plod along a little slower. *"For with you is the fountain of life; in your light we see light."* **Psalm 36:9**

I had better start thinking more about this than wallowing in my grief. Yes, the picture of my life as I see it now looks bleak. I am sad! Me, me, me! When will I get it through my head it (life) is not about me?

My faith has been on a rough ride. Lots of whys. Lots of anger. I'm old. I think too much. Why don't you think about being grateful for the support you have almost daily from family and friends? Think about that today instead of good "ole ME.

December 22, 2017

"Utterly meaningless! Everything is meaningless." **Ecclesiastes 1:2**

I have been living in a limbo. Unable to move forward; leaning into the past. The past pushes me away, but the future does also. Life is standing still for me; waiting for me to catch up. I'm tired. I want to wake up from this nightmare. Let's face it. I stopped living on March 28, 2016, also. The old me is gone.

The final chapters of my life are being written now. As I look, each page is blank. I must start living again.

December 23, 2017

"….I am the Light of the world; he who follows Me will not walk in darkness, but will have the Light of life." **John 8:12**

I am in a dark place and know that I'm not alone. During the holidays, millions of people are in darkness for a variety of reasons. Real misery doesn't love company. Knowing I share anguish with others doesn't lift me up an inch.

I own this spot, this place where I live. When I'm ready to move out, I will know it, and do it on my own, in my own time. Maybe one day I may see the Light is within me. In the dark place within me.

December 24, 2017

"The wound is the place where the light enters you." **—Rumi**

December 25, 2017

"Most important of all, continue to show deep love for each other, for love makes up for many of your faults." **Peter 4:8**

Grief can be an insidious thing. The impact it has on a grieving family is complex. The way we evolve in our grief and interact with one another isn't always comforting. Feelings are raw. Instead of warmth and comfort, distance and silence can prevail, unintentionally.

Christmas can be somewhat emotional under normal circumstances. Grief changes a family, and there can be an underlying tension.

There are no words to describe how surreal it feels. This life without Austin.

"Don't be afraid, for I have redeemed you; I have called you by name; you are mine. When you go through deep waters and great trouble, I will be with you..." **Isaiah 43:1-2**

"Storm's Wake" Pastel

Donna Grace

December 26, 2017

Fear is part of grief. Fear of change. Fear of loss. Fear of lost connections to family or friends. Fear of not feeling complete. Fear of permanent loss of happiness. Fear of being left in the past.

Where does this fear come from? Why is there fear after loss? It can lead to panic; wanting to run away. Do we fear our changed lives, and its finality? Are we fearful of living when our loved one is not?

I would gladly trade my life for my grandson's. I am the oldest in our family. The natural order would have the young surviving the old. Logical, but then there is the worst fear: Life gets the natural order wrong.

December 27, 2017

The holidays. Dreaded times for some of us who are grieving. Awkward times. We are encouraged to enjoy them. Feel guilty if we don't, and somewhat relieved when they are over.

I know I must seem different to my grandchildren, although I try to be the same as I was. You would think this tragedy, this loss, would bring us closer. Everyone is hurting in some way. Sometimes, it's easier to be quiet; to seek solitude.

In the first few months after Austin's death, we did talk more, show more love to one another. Now, we've retreated into our own worlds. It's as though there's nothing left to say. We've used up all the words that describe how we feel. What's the point of talking about it anymore?

It's been over thirty years since my sons' father, my husband and best friend, died. Taken away in a senseless accident like our sweet boy, Austin. He's missed so much in these years that have followed his death. Seeing his sons' sporting events, high school and college graduations, weddings, and grandchildren.

The good times. But, there were some not so good times. I needed him then, and I need him now more than ever. Strong shoulders to lean on. Someone with a perspective similar to mine. Reassuring words to comfort us. He was my rock; the rudder that steadied us through life's challenges.

Could he be supporting us somehow? I'm still here, although some days I wonder why.

January 2, 2018

Winter has thrust itself upon us. The trees seem to be shivering as an icy wind grabs the few remaining leaves.

A new year is supposed to give us incentive to shake off bad habits; clear our minds. Resolutions. Goals. This determined spirit lasts a few weeks for some. Others see lasting change.

"For I know the plans I have for you," declares the Lord, *"plans to prosper you and not to harm you, plans to give you hope and a future."* **Jeremiah 29:11**

I've set my mind on taking better care of myself. Too often since Austin's death, I've thought, "So what! I don't care that much about living anyway." Self-pity. Lots of it. This is non-productive. I'm going to try another way. Prosper? We'll see.

January 4, 2018

I've been thinking about the discomfort or tension I feel during family gatherings. Nothing like the holidays for self-reflection and a new year to inspire emotional growth.

Our family unit has changed dramatically. Where there were twin boys full of life, beloved, and a brilliant light in our lives, there is now a gaping hole where Austin was. When we're together as a family, we all see it, and feel it, but we say little about it. I need for this to change somewhat. We need to acknowledge him more. Say his name. It's not going to hurt more to hear it. It hurts when I don't hear it.

Each of us in Austin's family is going through grief at a different pace. It sickens me when I look at our reality. Our world blown up.

January 6, 2018

Is it really only the sixth day of the month? One frozen day followed by another. It takes some effort to be cheerful on cold, gray winter days under what I consider normal circumstances. That is, not having your world turned upside down by the loss of a child. I would like to burrow into the ground and hibernate, but as a human, this is not an option.

How did I get through last winter? I have no recollection at all. Grief has a way of blurring your view. Past and present. It is formidable. Lumbering along, this glacier-like creature, grief. Heavy, cold. Moving so slowly it's undetectable, but changing the landscape underneath. Me. My family.

January 13, 2018

As I look out my window this morning, I see ice and snow. Winter's gift. No thanks. I'm already uncomfortable just living the life I have now.

If I were in the warmth and sunshine of a tropical locale, I would still feel the same. There would just be a much better view. So, I guess it's about perspective. A lousy perspective doesn't care where you are or what the weather is like.

Through reading, I am encouraged to trust God and see my life and life's events through His perspective. This "life" is just a tiny speck compared to heavenly eternity we're promised. However, the tiny speck feels more like a boulder resting on my chest.

My perspective is being fed by how I feel now. Trust. This little word, a belief, that is supposed to lift the boulder. While the leap of faith is working in slow motion, it still sucks to be me.

January 20, 2018

Be strong and courageous…..for the Lord your God goes with you; he will never leave you or forsake you. **Deuteronomy 31:6**

Possibly, on the occasional day I'm not dragging my feet, I am being strong and courageous. Honestly, though, it feels more like avoidance, as I am willing myself not to think about "It." I may burst if I continue on my sad path. Sometimes, when my mind starts to go there, I push the thoughts away before they take ahold. Maybe this is being strong. Or, just survival kicking into gear.

Not many people die from a broken heart. It does take courage to go on and not give in to hopelessness from heartbreaking loss.

January 25, 2018

Grief can create out of control moments. Panic and fear roll over you, and knock you down as you watch your old life dissolve. The security of your former, predictable life is gone. Forever. Accepting this seems impossible. Accepting the death of one we love, how cruel.

There must be peace in acceptance. That is further down the road for me. However, a drop or two of acceptance is seeping through the crack of my stubborn mind.

Accept where you are today, Donna.

To shine on those living in darkness and in the shadow of death, to guide our feet into the path of peace.

—Luke 1:79

"Through the Shadows" Pastel

Donna Grace

January 29, 2018

Over the past few days, I've been leveling out a bit. However, the gray cloud still hangs over me as I begin each new day. What's happening? Is this slight change something to count on, trust? If I continue on this path, I will be giving in to reality. I have been fighting against this thing (acceptance) for a long time. In acceptance, is there a different pain waiting for me? Is this storm, the sickening, frightening part of grief over? Its grip on me has been steady and fierce. Which one of us is losing ground? I won't decide the outcome of that battle today.

"If patience is worth anything, it will endure to the end of time.

And a living faith will last in the midst of the blackest storm."

—Mahatma Gandhi

"After the Storm" Pastel

February 3, 2018

When we lose a loved one either suddenly or gradually from an illness, we think a lot about the fairness of it all. Why us? Even though I know there is no answer to the why, I still after almost two years of grieving, fall back into the never-ending question. Like a child, I want an answer.

I think we've been cheated out of our time with Austin. This makes me angry. We are taught to be fair; to treat others fairly. Life doesn't care about any of this. It doesn't keep score. I do. As if that helps.

"My argument against God was that the universe seemed so cruel and unjust. But how had I got this idea of just and unjust? A man does not call a line crooked unless he has some idea of a straight line. What was I comparing this universe with when I called it unjust?" **—C.S. Lewis**

February 7, 2018

I have started to notice a slight change on awakening in the morning. Before this awful thing happened, waking up in the morning was just that. Waking up. Starting my day. After our world exploded, I would have to make an adjustment on awakening. A sickening feeling would sink into my confused mind. Oh my God, this is my life now; having to reset every day to this hideous fact.

After almost two years, my mind has finally relented and let reality find a place beside wishful thinking. Reality, as horrible as it can be, has finally started to weave its way into my being. This process has been slow and very difficult. I'm a realist. I know I have a long road ahead of me.

Letting go of my old life. Letting go of my earthly hold on Austin.

February 9, 2018

There is another part of grief that I haven't really touched on. This monster, grief, has rolled over Austin's entire family. Those of us who loved him are suffering in our own private ways. Each of our losses is different, but the common thread is pain. There is no escaping it.

Seeing those you love suffering from loss is crippling when you know nothing can be done to lessen their pain. I look at our individual lives being blown apart. There is no way of fixing any of it.

The layers of our grief are complicated, and have a rippling effect that may take decades to smooth out. Why is my family being put through this? Again, with the "whys!" Do some just have better luck?

There seems to be no rhyme or reason to life. The erratic way it behaves. I look to God for strength, but some days the signal is weak.

I am the light of the world. Whoever follows me will never walk in darkness, but will have the light of life.

—John 8:12

"Abiding Harvest" Acrylic

February 10, 2018

".....But he said to them, where is your faith?" **Luke 8:25**

My faith has seen more changes in the last two years than a chameleon on a partly cloudy day. God gave these interesting creatures a built-in mechanism to adapt to their surroundings. A reliable safety-net for protection, moment by moment, day after day.

As humans are, according to scripture, the crown of His creation, where is our safety-net? The chameleon's is simple. You can see it! Ours, obscure. Ours is faith; this intangible thing we are to understand and adapt on our own.

Yes, there are churches, the bible, scholars of the scripture, and other deep thinkers who can help us. Practicing our faith, or not having any faith, is easy when life is going smoothly. Then, an event or a series of events take our safe world into one we no longer recognize.

When there is trouble, faith for some, kicks into high gear. Others may feel empty. Alone. Some of us reach for faith, but it eludes us; a conviction, difficult to grasp, as the mind and heart are not in sync.

Have patience, Donna. You're not going to figure everything out. Sometimes there isn't an answer you can easily see.

We are saved by trusting. And trusting means looking forward to getting something we don't have—for a man who already has something doesn't need to hope and trust that he will get it. But if we must keep trusting God for something that hasn't happened yet, it teaches us to wait patiently and confidently. **Romans 8:24-25**

February 12, 2018

It's a sunny morning, still cold, still winter. I feel very blah today. Flat. Blankly staring out my window. I picture myself as a cartoon character; Wile E. Coyote lying flat under a boulder. I have a perplexed look on my face. "What happened?" The giant steamroller of grief has left me flat. Life has been pushed out of me.

My daydream takes me further. Now, I'm in a car with only one gear, neutral. I step on the gas but go nowhere. I can't move forward or backward.

If I could get my car going, I would drive and drive. For days or months until I was safely back in my old life. But instead, I'm just sitting here. The radio doesn't even work.

Sometimes I wonder why I feel so all alone.
I wish I could just pack my bags and go home.
I'm getting lost in a thousand yesterdays.
After all this time and pain, I still can't find my way.
There's a road going somewhere,
There's a road leading somewhere,
Far away from here.
—John Rapp

"Going Home" Acrylic

February 15, 2018

"So, with you; Now is the time of your grief, but I will see you again and you will rejoice, and no one will take away your joy." **John 16:22**

Austin is gone from this earth, but our memories will live with us. That's what's left. "Now is the time of our grief." When I lie down to sleep at night, I know my grief will be there in the morning. "But I will see you again…." I believe this. These words have gotten me through many dark days. I hold on to this promise.

"When this tent we live in—our body here on earth is torn down, God will have a house in heaven for us to live in, a home he made, which will last forever." **Revelation 7:9**

February 18, 2018

You will keep in perfect peace him whose mind is steadfast, because he trusts in you. **Isaiah 26:3**

While grieving, I have thought about eventually feeling at peace. Will I ever be at peace with my new life? Before I can have peace, I need to figure out what it really is. I know what it isn't. Achievement. Feeling peace after reaching a goal or a stage in life. I foolishly thought I would become more at peace as I got older, wiser. Nope. Didn't happen.

I remember when my boys were teenagers, I would lie awake at night unable to sleep until I heard their car pull into the driveway. A sense of peace would come over me, then, I could relax and go to sleep. This peace hinged on things falling into place.

Finding any peace through hard times or devasting loss takes enormous trust. I trust God. However, if I had total, complete, deep in my soul trust, I would see the world differently. I would see my life differently. And, I would see the loss of our sweet boy differently.

February 20, 2018

We are being gifted by a beautiful morning. The sky is clear, birds are singing. Spring is gently stepping into winter's domain. Tiny, green spears of daffodils are piercing through brown leaves and pine needles. There's a change in the air so slight, but detectable to nature's family. Plants, animals, and even humans.

I'm changing also. The change is so gradual that I barely notice, but it is there. I can sense it. The weight of my grief is shifting. The suffocating grip is loosening. Grief is evolving. I'm not sure to what, but I'm thankful for the change, even though it is slight.

I don't spend enough time being thankful to God. Thankfulness in the chaos of grief is difficult to say the least. To achieve a consistent, thankful persona during grief starts with surrendering feelings of anger toward God. This is taking me a long time. To put it mildly, I think my family has been given the short end of the stick. How could I possibly be thankful when I look at what we've lost?

Practice being thankful for the little things, Donna. The list will grow given time and effort. We all like to be thanked when we've done something for someone.

It would be impossible to wrap my mind around all that God gives me every moment of every day.

And I pray that you, being rooted and established in love, may have power, together with all saints to grasp how wide and long and high and deep is the love of Christ, and to know this love surpasses knowledge. **Ephesians 3:16-19**

February 24, 2018

"I'm living in my worst nightmare." My sister spoke these words to me after her beautiful, young daughter died in a senseless accident over twenty years ago. Her words stayed with me as I cried for her and prayed it wouldn't happen to me. Now, I'm living in my worst nightmare. "I will counsel you and watch over you." I imagine most of us take the "watch over you" part of this verse too literally. When something horrible happens to us we think, "Weren't you supposed to be watching over us?" Yet, shit happens!! Plenty of it, and it makes us angry and disappointed in God. He let us down. He allowed us to enter our worst nightmare.

No matter how many ways I look at these terrible tragedies in our family or all senseless suffering, it eventually returns to trust. Trust in the Lord and stop trying to figure it out. You're not going to find the answer with the knowledge you're equipped with now.

When you've been flattened by grief, your strength wavers day by day. Somehow, I manage to crawl out of the hole in which I begin every day. My sister is surviving her worst nightmare, and most likely, I will too.

February 28, 2018

It was good being out of my routine for a couple of days. Time spent away from home with friends can be rejuvenating in a way. However, I am back to my regular life, and it doesn't feel that great. My reality, my unreal life that is my new normal, is here waiting for me to take up where I left off. Grief is so confusing and unpredictable. One day I feel almost passable, the next day I'm back in the middle of my sad place. Just as I see a little light around the edges, down I go.

I have wondered since I have been at this for almost two years, if I am conditioning myself to feel bad. Do I even remember how not hurting feels? This is an unsettling thought.

I see myself on a road trip with no map. I may be on the right road, but I'm not sure. It's been a while since I was at my destination, so something that was familiar now looks strange and out of place. It's dark, so I can't get my bearings. No landmarks to show the way.

I know God is waiting for me to ask for help. Some days I'm stubborn and want to follow my path.

You are my lamp, O Lord, the Lord turns my darkness into light. **2 Samuel 22:29**

March 1, 2018

I used to look forward to this day. Spring isn't officially here, but it is announcing the arrival in colorful ways. Winter's heavy blanket has been cast aside to expose delicate, green sprouts of life. Bright splotches of yellow daffodil and forsythia wake up the brown landscape. Soft, pastel hues of pink and lavender color trees that were bare yesterday. Nature is in a rush to get things underway.

This was my favorite time of year. Renewal. Winter's sleep was over. Now, spring is tainted with sad memories. Austin's last days. Our second-year anniversary is approaching. Grief and sadness obscure happy memories.

I'm not preventing myself from moving forward in my grief, but I cannot will myself to feel better. There are no longer stretches of gut-wrenching agony. It's become a dull ache. Persistent, annoying. Why can't I just feel whole again! The battle within continues. Reality and acceptance duking it out with denial.

Accept that you're are not going to feel whole again, Donna. My own words written in this journal the second month of grief: "I pray the hole in my heart, the emptiness, will scab over. That nothing will fill it. It's Austin's place. His spot."

My perception of feeling whole will mature into something. I don't know what that is yet.

In Him was Life and Life was the light of men. And light shines on in the darkness for the darkness has never overpowered it. **John 1:4-5**

March 17, 2018

Find rest, O my soul, in God alone; my hope comes from him. He alone is my rock and my salvation; he is my fortress. I will not be shaken. **Psalm 62:5-6**

I went to the cemetery yesterday. Even though I visit often, as I drove through the quiet garden, I felt out of place. Why am I here? Still unreal, still baffling. As I approached Austin's place, a service was in progress. Surreal memories flooded my mind.

A soldier was being laid to rest. I stopped my car and waited. After a while, three rifle shots broke the stillness, followed by taps' farewell. This poignant moment filled me with melancholy.

Most times I visit, I'm alone in the quiet, and I just sit on our bench and try to wrap my mind around why I'm there. Somedays, children's voices waft through the air. A school, brimming with life, is nearby. Ironically, it was the boys' middle school. Their eight-grade graduation was in the church across the street. How cruel life can be. Each marker at the cemetery represents a life ended and someone's broken heart.

The widow or mother of the soldier clutched the folded flag to her chest as she got into the car that would take her from this place of sorrow and loss. I knew where she was going. I've been there for almost two years. Her sad place.

March 21, 2018

You will show me the path of life; your presence is fullness of joy; at your right hand are pleasures forevermore. **Psalm 16:11**

Even if I didn't have a calendar, I would know it was March. It's not warm enough for the grass to be green, or even trees. Though the early blossoms of fruit trees and bushes add color, the quieter hues of winter still dominate the landscape. A warm day will turn chilly the next. Back and forth, unable to commit either way.

Nature knows where it's going. There is no doubt whatsoever. It instinctively follows "the path of life." Humans, need help with this. Our instinct is to survive; to live. Finding God's path of life requires effort.

Some days it's an effort just to write in this journal. To stay in my routines. To answer my phone. To be out and about participating in life.

I've come a long way from the hysteria and heart wrenching sickness of March, 2016. But, I'm not on God's path of life. I know God is cutting me little slack. I'm aware. I want to live again; not just be alive. I want to experience fullness of joy. The kind of joy that resides deep in my soul. Joy that remains with me through all the seasons of life.

"Just Around the Bend" Pastel

March 22, 2018

"I'm just sad." How many times have I said this over the last two years? I am looking at life through a veil. My former clear and bright life is now blurred with sadness.

The mind is a restless and complex thing. It can make or break a day. If I could let God's light permeate this veil, my days would be much easier. My mind is stubborn, and wants to be in control. It has its own plans. I know in my heart this is not what I should do. I ask myself, "How does this continuous sadness honor Austin? Is his spirit gratified by my constant suffering?"

While daydreaming earlier today, an image popped into my mind. I was on a cruise liner in the middle of the ocean. My view was from the back of the ship. I thought about accidently falling over the side into the deep blue world of the sea; watching in horror as the ship cruised away. Treading water in unfathomable depths. Hopeless and alone in giant swells of water.

A tiny boat behind a wall of blue green appears. A rope is thrown to me. There is no hesitation or fear of who is saving me. I grab on. I trust. Why is it so hard for me to see God's life line that is offered to me moment by moment, day after day?

March 25, 2018

The righteous cry out, and the Lord hears them; he delivers them from all their troubles. The Lord is close to the brokenhearted and saves those who are crushed in spirit. **Psalm 34:17-18**

Living with a broken heart. I remember saying shortly after Austin died that I would have to learn how to live with a broken heart. I know it is broken; certain that it is completely broken. I've said my heart was broken many times throughout my life. It's mended over time, but the years have taken their toll. When I break an object and repair it, I know that it will show to some extent its flaw. It may be functional again but also fragile.

As I write, I see a large vase in my living room. I remember the day Austin and Clayton were running through the house, and the vase was accidentally knocked over. I recognize now I had placed a value on the vase that exceeded its real importance. However, I was horrified as it broke in half. But, I wasn't going to give up on it; throw it away. I knew I could fix it, and I did. If I positioned it just so, I couldn't see where it was cracked.

I can't fix my broken heart. It still beats, and that's got to be good enough for now.

My vase is another reminder of the past. When I dust it, I remember the day it was broken. Cracked, but useable. Fragile, yet memorable.

March 28, 2018

The Last Goodbye

As you go your way, may peace walk with you

Until the adjoining day!

And when that day comes,

With early morning's hue,

While walking on grass, beaded

With drops of dew,

May peace still walk with you.

Oh, this pain about my heart

That harbors all my wants and cares,

How I would like to tear it from my flesh,

And end these painful years.

But for the hope of eternal love,

Given to those completing God's task,

I can for another moment endure

These painful throbs about my chest.

—T.K. Sparkman

March 29, 2018

Yesterday marked two years without our boy. When I look back at that hideous week after his death, I wonder how I'm still here today.

Relatives from near and far gathered with us for comfort and support. Having family and friends to assist with the basic things that needed to be done was very helpful. Nevertheless, the stress level was amplified by the varying degree of emotion we each possessed. It didn't go as smoothly as I had assumed it would. I was no help at all. I was in a parallel world watching a horror movie. Unable to move, turn it off, or return to reality.

During the tumultuous time after a death, some families crack under the pressure. My family survived that week in hell, but we were not unscathed.

Who is a God like you, who pardons sin and forgives the transgression of the remnant of his inheritance? You do not stay angry forever, but delight to show mercy.

You will again have compassion on us; you will tread our sins underfoot and hurl all our iniquities into the depths of the sea. **Micah 7:18-19**

April 1, 2018 (Easter Sunday)

O, Jacob, O Israel, how can you say that the Lord doesn't see your troubles and isn't being fair? Don't you yet understand? Don't you know by now that the everlasting God, the Creator of the farthest parts of the earth never grows faint or weary? No one can fathom the depths of his understanding. He gives power to the tired and worn out, and strength to the weak. Even youths shall be exhausted, and young men will all give up. But they that wait upon the Lord shall renew their strength. They shall mount up with wings like eagles; they shall run and not be weary; they shall walk and not be faint. **Isaiah 40:27-31**

April 3, 2018

"But they that wait upon the Lord shall renew their strength." Does this mean if I just have patience while I'm grieving, God will renew my strength? That eventually the pain will be bearable, and I will feel lighter. The hard part is waiting. I hurt now. I am weary and worn out.

Being patient with grief takes strength. Day after day adjusting to a life that is so hard to accept. It's easier to be angry and resentful to God and the random way life unfolds. In today's world, a lot of us want what we want right now. Speed is a virtue.

Life has different plans. Sooner or later it will throw something at us that we can't resolve quickly, or maybe, ever. I know God is renewing my strength. Some days it's easier to see and feel than others.

April 11, 2018

"And let the peace of God rule in your heart to which also you were called in one body; and be thankful." **Colossians3:15 (NKJV)**

I've been writing in this journal for almost two years. The first few months, my writing was clumsy and forced. It's easy to see the desperation in my handwriting. Thick and heavy lines scribbling sentences that struggled for coherence.

Journaling was just a waste of time and effort. Everything felt hopeless. I didn't want to live. Every day was agony. I knew I was standing at the edge of a bottomless, black hole. I was tempted to just step in; to escape. To be unconscious, floating in a dark void. I didn't think I had the strength to endure this enormous loss.

There was no epiphany. A light did not shine from above to rouse me from my "death." It was a gradual change. A slow awakening. I was angry at God for allowing my grandson to die, but also knew I needed help to get through each day. When loss brings you to your knees, you can remain there, or look up and begin praying.

As I read my journal from the beginning, I see the movement of grief shifting its position day by day. I write about its heaviness. I described it as a dense and enormous object. Immovable. I see it somewhat differently now; more fluid, as a liquid.

This substance, liquid, does not resist change of shape but does resist size. I think the size of my grief will stay with me, but the shape of it will change. Hopefully, it will become less tangled. Its form will become wider; the dark, deep depths of it will level out into reflecting, shallow pools.

This is where I want to go; what I picture for myself. I still struggle with grief, but not at the intensity of before. I haven't fully accommodated my new world, and am vulnerable to a grief wave. This is my life now. I adjust a little day by day. But some days, I fall back into the past. I stay for a little while but am realizing I don't belong there.

The more you love, the deeper your loss. Would I take back that love to spare myself this grief of unimaginable depth? Never!

April 14, 2018

Nineteen years ago, twin boys came into our world. Identical twins. They wore bracelets the first few months until we could find other ways to tell them apart. Austin was first born, a little bigger than Clayton. Throughout their years together, he remained slightly bigger, developing a more dominant personality. Clayton was usually more acquiescent, but there were still lots of disagreements. Yet, there was much more; a deep, connective love. It was as though they were living one, huge life together. Their high school football coach told them they shared the same brain. They laughed and enjoyed that assessment.

These last two birthdays have been surreal. It's hard to describe how I feel today. Empty, let down. What should be happy just isn't for me now. I will smile, though, and we will have cake and blow out candles. But, I will also take flowers to the cemetery. I will look at his marker and wonder again why things had to go so horribly wrong. Austin should be going to prom tonight. He should be graduating high school beside his brother.

These feelings are with me, and I can't deny them. They don't crush me, though, as I'm learning to move along a little more peaceably with grief. The anger is starting to wane. I'm exhausted from running a marathon for the past two years. Running away from grief and loss. I need to give in a little. I've accepted loss before in my life. Time will soften the pain.

"Come to me, all you who are weary and burdened, and I will give you rest. Take My yoke upon you and learn from Me, for I am gentle and humble in heart, and you will find rest for your souls. For My yoke is wholesome, and My burden is light and easy to be borne." **Matthew 11:28-30(AMP)**

When I was a girl, I didn't keep a diary. As an adult, I occasionally tried writing in a journal but would lose interest after a few days. My source of creativity has mostly been art but more as a hobby than vocation. Painting is therapeutic, in a way, as emotions and thoughts take form on canvas or paper. Since Austin's death, creating art was good for my mind as it took me away from my pain for stretches of time. I've read your brain can't concentrate on two different things at the same time.

While writing in my grief journal and painting, I noticed over time, my paintings were reflecting in some way the direction of my writing. Frequent words in my journal: paths, roads, light, darkness, and water were transformed into images through my painting.

I didn't set out to journal my grief experience and share those personal thoughts through publication. As I was writing, I found myself going back and reading what I had written. My original intention was not to do this as I thought it best to keep moving forward and not look back. However, I found it helpful to revisit previous days in grieving. I would forget an earlier insight or thought conclusion.

This book is just what the titles implies; a look at grief, my grief. Grief is as unique to the one who is grieving as the fingerprint. My grief will not be exactly as yours. There are many emotions I have in common with others who are grieving, though. When we're hurting, we may seek a support group. Sharing our problem and listening to others with a similar experience can bring a little relief. Perhaps, hearing a different perspective can result in new insight for our issue. That's what I'm offering. A little support.

I think of myself, my being, as a vessel; open to whatever I choose. Most of my earlier life I had a rather narrow view of the world and focused mostly on what was happening around me. Looking out for my family, myself, and things that were important to me. Happy being a wife and mother. Busy raising a family, chasing dreams. Then, the sudden death of my husband blew my safe world apart. I was stunned with grief and anger. It was a very difficult time. My boys were without a father, and I had no idea how to be a single parent of teenage boys.

Since Austin's death, I have opened my mind and heart to God. When my husband died, I wanted help from God, but was impatient and just wanted the pain to go away. I sought comfort in people and things.

The summer following Austin's death, I spent a lot of time reading spiritual books, meditating, praying, and thinking. I had little energy for much else. I was talking to God. A lot. I had broadened my awareness of him. Had I not done this, I would have missed the gift he gave me.

It was August, and summer was beginning to wear out its welcome. The days were hot and humid. At dusk, I would slather myself with insect repellant and venture out into my backyard. I used this slightly cooler time of day to water plants, admire my roses, and pull a few weeds from flower beds. This mindless task of weed pulling was soothing to me, and I loved the sounds of nature at twilight. The locust buzzing in a distant tree; a dove calling to its mate.

I had worked my way around the perimeter of my yard to an area of pine trees. The mostly shaded space, covered in pine needles, provided a dismal home for plants. A few determined weeds survived without regular watering.

I had a grip on my next victim and was about to yank, when I paused. There was enough light for me to see that it wasn't a weed. I brushed away layers of pine needles and looked closely. It was a tomato plant! I was in disbelief. How could this have happened? But, there it was; small, but large enough to have a few oddly shaped tomatoes.

God heard my prayers those endless days of grieving. Something extraordinary had happened. An ordinary thing became extraordinary. It took me a while to grasp its scope and meaning: A tomato plant growing in hard, clay soil where weeds barely survived. It seemed like a miracle to me.

God showed me his power, and how something can live and be productive in adverse conditions. This was my gift! A little plant convinced me that God does hear us, and if we open ourselves to his presence, we will see the uncommon in life's ordinary experiences.

Feeling and seeing the presence of God in my little space in the world lifted my spirit, but we don't get a free pass from grief. There is no express line to rush us through our pain. We have to just bear the unbearable.

Love is God's greatest gift to us. "For nothing loved is ever lost, and I have loved so much."

"Aubie's View"   Acrylic

AUSTIN JAMES SPICER
"AUBIE"

APRIL 14, 1999

TO

MARCH 28, 2016

LOVING SON, BROTHER AND FRIEND

OUR LOVE GOES WITH YOU AND

OUR SOULS WAIT TO JOIN YOU

"THINK OF ME AS LIVING IN THE HEARTS

OF THOSE I HAVE TOUCHED.

FOR NOTHING LOVED IS EVER LOST &

I HAVE LOVED SO MUCH."

PHILLIPIANS 3:14

I PRESS ON TOWARD THE GOAL TO WIN THE

PRIZE FOR WHICH GOD HAS CALLED ME

HEAVENWARD IN CHRIST JESUS

HOTTY TODDY

33

Printed in the United States
By Bookmasters